Rainbows
for Teachers

Rainbows
for Teachers

Janet Colsher Teitsort

BAKER BOOK HOUSE
Grand Rapids, Michigan 49516

ISBN: 0-8010-8905-0

Third printing, December 1993

Printed in the United States of America

Scripture quotations are from the King James Version (KJV), the New International Version (NIV), the Living Bible (LB), the Revised Standard Version (RSV), and the Good News Bible (GNB).

Dedicated to the
glory and honor of
the master teacher,
our Lord and Savior,
Jesus Christ,

and

to my husband,
John,
who has encouraged me
to pursue my dreams.

$\mathscr{C}$ontents

3 A Rainbow of Parents

4 A Rainbow of Golden Moments

$\mathscr{P}$reface

The joy of teaching is unique. The satisfaction is indescribably rewarding. But often amidst the lesson plans, grading, conferences, reports, and committee meetings we teachers lose sight of the teaching. We find ourselves bone weary, depleted emotionally, physically, and spiritually. This is the time to turn to the master teacher, our Lord and Savior, Jesus Christ. He alone can renew our commitment to teaching and give us strength for our daily task.

It is my hope that this book will uplift and encourage teachers and serve as a beacon pointing them to the one who gives insight and wisdom.

At the end of each section are "My Rainbows to Remember," journaling pages where you may record your joys and vent your frustrations. This will enable you to keep everything in proper perspective.

This book has been a pleasure to write. May it bless your teaching and your life as you discover your own rainbows. Remember, God is just a prayer away.

I express my heartfelt appreciation to those who have assisted with this work in any way. I will always cherish their prayerful support, time, and encouragement. God bless all of you.

PART ONE

A Rainbow of Teaching

*And seeing the multitudes, he went up into a mountain;
and when he was set, his disciples came unto him; and he
opened his mouth and taught them.*

Matthew 5:1, 2 KJV

*For the LORD sees not as man sees; man looks on
the outward appearance, but the LORD looks on the
heart.*

1 Samuel 16:7 RSV

Crayon Drawings

They come bearing gifts
of crayon drawings.
Sometimes,
I barely have time to notice.
"Uh-huh,
that's nice.
Lay it on my desk."
   I'll toss it away after school.

But today I looked at them.
And I thought,
   These are treasures.
These children
have given me
the richness
of their hearts.

Flowers appear on the earth;
the season of singing has come.

Song of Songs 2:12 NIV

The Coronation

The shy little fella,
head bowed,
thrust it toward me.
Thanking him,
I oohed and aahed
over it.
"Dandelions
always make me think
of dots of gold,"
I said.

The next recess
they came by the handfuls,
long stem,
short stem,
no stem.

I sat there
reigning.
I had just been
proclaimed
"Dandelion Queen."

And let us not grow weary in well-doing, for in due season we shall reap, if we do not lose heart.

Galatians 6:9 RSV

*I*n His Strength

It has been a hard day,
Father,
   a hurry-up-go-fast-
     one-step-forward-
slide-back-two
day.
Do all of your children
have days like that,
or just teachers?

When lesson plans beg
to be written, and the
grading is piled high,
or the office calls
for a report past due,
and I can't find it,
let me not grow weary.

When it seems I am
making little progress
with a student, and a
thankless parent voices
his complaint,
help me
not to lose heart.

But remind me that
if I keep on keeping on,
trusting in *your* strength,
the day of reaping will come.

Peace I leave with you; my peace I give you.

John 14:27 NIV

The Encumbrance

Round and round it goes,
this merry-go-round
of committee meetings,
forms, reports.
Is this what I was called
to do?

I know things
need to be done.
But in their
quest for excellence,
don't let schools
defeat their purpose.
Remind them
not to lose
the *teach*
in the teacher.

Father, forgive
my complaining.
Renew my
stressed-out mind.
Relax my
fatigued body.
Release me
into your peace.

Look carefully how you walk, not as unwise men
but as wise, making the most of the time.
Ephesians 5:15, 16 RSV

Planning Time

Hot sweaty bodies
fidget in line,
eager for a drink
after recess.

But today I
have more patience.
Today I smile
more easily.
Today I
have a prep.

As I stand guard
at the fountain,
my thoughts
roller-skate
ahead, organizing
my work time—
    return the library books,
    pick up the bulletin-board paper,
    check my mailbox . . .

not one precious
second to waste.

Lord, stretch my
prep like the
rubber bands on
our geo-boards.
Expand my time
in every direction.

If I pass a
co-worker
in the hall,
remind me to
keep my
greeting short.
There will be
time to
visit later.

When I stop
in the lounge
for a refreshment
break, don't let
me sit down.
I might stay.

May the promise
of a lighter
work load tonight,

and a relaxed
day tomorrow,
keep me on task.

Grant me your
wisdom in
making the
most of my
time.

*This is the assurance we have in approaching God:
that if we ask anything according to his will, he
hears us. And if we know that he hears us—what-
ever we ask—we know that we have what we asked
of him.*

1 John 5:14, 15 NIV

Intercession

Heartache
pounds
in my chest
as I witness
the daily
struggles of
my students.

Shattered spirits,
maimed by
adults who
have made
wrong choices,
strive to survive.

Illness clutches
the weak in body,
refusing to be
shaken off.

Others grasp
at the
knowledge
that seems
to elude them.

I see a mosaic
of their needs
and I cry
out to you
for solutions.

What a powerhouse
you provided
when you gave
the gift of prayer!

I marveled
when you
prompted me
to pray for
each student
individually.

How wise
you were
to guide me
to rotate
my prayer
list daily.

Your answers
revolutionized
my classroom,
and I stand in
awe to watch
you work.

I have opened a door to you that no one can shut.

Revelation 3:8 LB

ℐhrough Open Doors

The end of a day,
and what a day
it has been, Father—
a convocation,
a captured tick,
and a swallowed coin,
all mixed in among
the academic.

These situations
cause me to chuckle—
a person has to be
a little crazy to teach.
Yet, there is no
question how
I arrived here.
Before I was
born, you placed
the gift of
teaching within me.

In your perfect
timing you
awakened
the desire.

To those who
scoff at such
a notion, I
wish I had
a videotape
of my life.

You are a God
who opens doors.

Professors cried,
"No jobs, seek
another field."
You fanned the
flame of faith,
increasing my
determination.

It was not
by chance
a teacher retired.
I recognized
your hand
opening the
door to employment.

Father, thank you
for the open doors.
Help me to
walk worthy of
your high calling.

He will not break the bruised reed, nor quench the dimly burning flame. He will encourage the fainthearted, those tempted to despair.

Isaiah 42:3 LB

Renew a right spirit within me.

Psalm 51:10 KJV

ℛekindle Me

Days stretch
as infinite as
our number line,
smothering me
with their sameness.

A calendar laden
with
    committees to meet,
    conferences to be held,
    convocations to attend
quenches my vitality.

Mounds of
    papers to grade,

plans to be written,
preparations to complete
snuff out my joy.

A feeling of
"Who really cares?"
dampens my spirit.

For a moment
I fantasize about
escaping into the
perfect day framed
in my window,
but I know I cannot.

How did this
happen to me?
I, who love
teaching, should not
be experiencing this
virus of discontent.

A variable depression,
the malaise of burnout,
works havoc in my life.

Father, what is
the antidote for
this malady?
Grade level changes?

Another career?
Hanging on?
What is the solution?
Must the change
come from within?

Renew a right
spirit within me,
O Lord.

Regenerate my attitude
until it is one of thankfulness
    for an opportunity
    to touch lives,
        for health enabling
        me to work,
                and for a vocation
                in a free land.

Rekindle me, Lord.
Make the love
I first had
for teaching
flame brightly
again.

Listen when I reprimand you; I will give you good advice and share my knowledge with you.

Proverbs 1:23 GNB

iscipline

Blatant disrespect
blares from
T.V. sitcoms,
portraying rudeness
as the way to act.

Parents, seeking a
scapegoat for
their child's problems,
bind the teacher's
control with threats.

Children
    bounced between
    weary caretakers
rebel at authority, and
permissiveness reigns.

Lord, as we
begin a new
year, show me
the plan of
discipline that
I should use.

Help me to
model myself
after you,
disciplining
with love.
Keep me
fair and
consistent.

May this
classroom
be a stabilizing
influence on
these students
living in an
ever-changing
world.

Commit everything you do to the Lord. Trust him to help you do it and he will.

Psalm 37:5 LB

Mastery

Short attention spans,
created by the
quick-change stimuli
of the electronic age,
cause me to gear up
to capture the focus
of my students.

As I manipulated
the puppets, teaching
a phonics lesson,
the children were
unwittingly learning.

Intent on their
task, they worked
fervently.

Then it happened.

Small hands sprang
together in an
overture of applause,
when in my best
puppet voice
Andy Muppet
succeeded.

A sweeping
glance revealed
understanding
had dawned.
Facial horizons
broke into smiles
of pleasure.

I, too, rejoiced.
In that moment
of mastery, my
labor was rewarded.

For moments of
victory, I give
you thanks,
Lord.

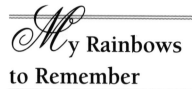

My Rainbows
to Remember

Rewards given to me by my students:

My feelings about the highs and lows of teaching:

Areas of teaching I want to work on:

A successful teaching experience I want to remember:

The times I've felt most frustrated about teaching:

PART TWO

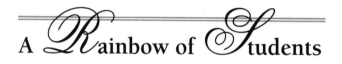

A Rainbow of Students

Even a child is known by his actions, by whether his conduct is pure and right.

Proverbs 20:11 NIV

I knew you before you were formed within your mother's womb.

Jeremiah 1:5 LB

God's Unique Designs

Each year these
pint-sized personalities
enter my classroom,
enriching my life.

Like opening a
new box of
crayons and being
delighted by the
array of colors,
I am intrigued
by the yearly
spectrum of students.

Father, what a
master Creator
you are!
Designed by you,
your children arrive
from the womb

with physical characteristics
and temperaments intact.

Daily circumstances
tint their lives,
adding depth
to their characters.
At last, they
begin their pilgrimage
through school.

How exciting it is
when they arrive
at my door,
for I am a teacher,
and I perceive
the promise
you have sketched
for each life.

Our time together
speeds by as if
it is a
fast-forwarding
video.

In the passing
years, I catch
momentary glimpses
of them as they

scurry about
school activities.

Recognizing
the personalities,
I marvel to
see how their
colors unfold
upon the rainbow
canvases of their lives.

Father, thank you
for touching my
life with the
uniqueness of
your children.

So faith, hope, love abide, these three; but the greatest of these is love.

1 Corinthians 13:13 RSV

Students of Years Gone By

Year after year
they drop by
for a hug, a smile,
for affirmation that
I still remember
and care.

When they appear at my door,
I am transformed by joy.
Just as they glowed
when I gave them
"warm fuzzies"
for achievement,
I beam to see my rewards.

More than academic success
was accomplished during
our time together.
Faith was challenged,

hope was stirred,
and now love abides.

Father, bless these
students
of years gone by, these
teachers
of my heart.
And go gently
with them through life.

And behold a leper came to him and knelt before him, saying, "Lord, if you will, you can make me clean." And he stretched out his hand and touched him.

Matthew 8:2, 3 RSV

Stretch out My Hand

She comes and lays her
matted head against me.
I halfheartedly hug her.
Inside, I silently pray,
    Please don't let her have lice.

After she's gone
I chide myself
for holding back.
I hope she didn't notice,
but I suspect she did.
    Children always notice.

Tears spring to my eyes.
I promise myself that
the next time
I will completely

envelop her
in my arms.

Father, why can't I be
more like Jesus?
He touched
the unlovely; he
reached right out
and touched the leper,
and he was healed.

I'll bet a bear hug would
go a long way toward
healing this little waif.

Help me to
overcome this
barrier from within.
Help me to be
more like the
master teacher.

When the trumpets sounded, the people shouted,
and at the sound of the trumpet, when the people
gave a loud shout, the wall collapsed.

Joshua 6:20 NIV

The Survivor

He comes racing
into the classroom,
issuing forth
motor noises,
honking loudly,
sideswiping
anyone who dares
to get in his way.

He has arrived,
this classroom terror.
Already the day
stretches forth
unbearable.

Battered by parents
caught up in
their own trauma,
he has learned
to survive.

Brick by brick,
he laid the wall,
barricading himself
from his abusive world.
Now he is a
prisoner within.

Once or twice,
I've removed a brick—
moments when I've
gone the extra mile.
In response,
he came to me,
a frightened little
boy who desperately
wanted to love
and be loved.

Guide me, Father.
Use me as *your*
instrument—
your trumpet,
to tear down walls.

A merry heart maketh a cheerful countenance.
Proverbs 15:13 *KJV*

The Joyful Child

Packaged by you
with the
gift of laughter,
this child
springs into
my classroom
with a
merry heart.

Like a
helium-filled
balloon,
her laughter
rises from
within, lifting
our hearts to
the realm of
merriment.

A day of
lightheartedness
lies before us.

Father, thank
you for this
child and her
cheerful
countenance.

Therefore judge nothing before the appointed time;
wait till the Lord comes. He will bring to light what
is hidden in darkness and will expose the motives of
men's hearts.

1 Corinthians 4:5 NIV

Misjudged

This whiny child has
given me fits.
Sometimes I've wanted
to scream.

The parents have
repeatedly told me,
"We can't figure
it out. There isn't
any reason for him
to be like that."

Today they say
they are getting
a divorce.

Now I see.

Now I understand.

The darkness has
been gathering
all year.

My heart goes out
to this child, Father.
Comfort him,
enable him to cope.

Help me to
remember there is
always a reason.

And Jesus went forth, and saw a great multitude,
and was moved with compassion toward them, and
he healed their sick.

Matthew 14:14 KJV

Lamentations

Time after time
this little waif
appears at my
side bearing
complaints—

    headaches,
       stomachaches,
             hangnails,

    vague,
      varied,
           constant.

Silently I search
the pale blue
eyes for reason.

Is it temperament?
Is it a cry for attention?
Is it the body's way
of dealing with stress?

Sometimes I just
want to say,
"Go sit down."

Then I think of
you, Jesus, the
master teacher.

The crowds
pressed you
on every side,
always demanding.

Maybe you
wanted to tell
them to go sit
down, too;
but you didn't.

Instead, you
looked on
them with
eyes of
compassion
and took care
of their needs.

Bestow your
wisdom on
me. Let me
see her through
your eyes.

Help me to
remember
not to negate
her pain,
but to apply
the healing
properties
of a Band-Aid,
or a wet
paper towel,
accompanied
by a hug
and a smile.

But he raises up the needy out of affliction, and
makes their families like flocks.

Psalm 107:41 RSV

Shepherd Her, Lord

A purple barrette
clasps a wisp
of fine hair
perched atop
a face sprinkled
with freckles.

Questioning eyes,
framed in circlets
of blue-gray sorrow,
peer out at me.

We are reading
one-on-one.

Pausing, she leans
over and whispers,
"My mommy's
in jail, and no
one wants me."

Shaken,
I listen,
as her pain
spills out.

I ask myself,
    What comfort can I give?
    My arms for the moment?
    My heart of love?
But what about
the nights and
the weekends?
What about next
week, or next year?

Silently I pray.
Jesus, come and
enfold this child;
shelter her in your
shepherding arms.

How much better to get wisdom than gold, to choose understanding rather than silver!

Proverbs 16:16 NIV

The Diligent

Woven within
the tapestry
of my class,
diligent students
sparkle like
iridescent threads,
accenting the
school year.

Motivated
intrinsically,
they strive
for perfection—
demanding little
and giving much.

Quietly they enter
the classroom.
Quickly they
set about
their tasks.

Cubicles filled
with their
belongings
reveal
systematic minds.

Maturity and
responsibility
are their
companions.
Possessing a
keen sense of
right, their
behavior is
without fault.

Assignments
turned in
promptly
contain
letters and
numerals
standing at
attention on
crisp sheets
of school paper.

They are every
teacher's dream—
these students

who latch onto
wisdom at such
an early age.

But their qualities
make them easy
to overlook.

When those
who have
special needs
make excessive
demands on
my time,
don't let me
neglect the
diligent students.

Help me to
remember
they need
encouragement,
too.

Father, bless
these children
who do their best.

I press on toward the goal.

Philippians 3:14 RSV

Let us run with perseverance the race that is set before us.

Hebrews 12:1 RSV

*P*ressing On

Seconds drag on
as students stumble
over words
they read
proficiently
yesterday.

How can this be,
Father?

I see the
bewilderment
in their eyes
that seem to say,
"I knew it
yesterday,
but today
I forget."

Grant me
patience
with these
children
who struggle
to achieve.

Fill me with
your compassion.
Make my concern
be for their
plight and
not my own.

Help me to
bear this
torturing
pace.

Let my voice
ring with
encouragement
instead of criticism.
Remind me to
treat them with
dignity and sensitivity.

Father, prompt me
to affirm each student
with praise.
Keep me persevering,
pressing on toward
the goal.

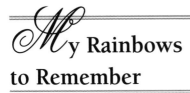

My Rainbows
to Remember

Special children whom I will always remember:

Needy children who touched my heart:

Diligent students whom I will always remember:

Joyful students who brightened my day:

Gifted students who challenged me:

PART THREE

A Rainbow of Parents

*Fathers, do not exasperate your children; instead, bring
them up in the training and instruction of the Lord.*

Therefore, as God's chosen people, holy and dearly loved, clothe yourselves with compassion, kindness, humility, gentleness and patience.

Colossians 3:12 NIV

The First Day

I stand at the door
gathering them in.
Their eyes meet mine,
and I see
their apprehension.

Uttering words
of reassurance,
I pin their dinosaur
name tags on
and usher them
to their niche
for the next
nine months.

Turning, I look
at the parents.
I see

a thousand questions
etched
on their faces.

Will she care?
Will she love?
Will she understand?

Calm their fears.
Let them see me
clothed with
your kindness,
Lord.

May they recognize
your compassion
within me,
reaching out,
encircling their
children with gentleness,
on this
the first day of school.

*I appeal to you, brothers, in the name of our Lord
Jesus Christ, that all of you agree with one another
so that there may be no divisions among you and
that you may be perfectly united in mind and
thought.*

1 Corinthians 1:10 NIV

Building Bridges

They are going to be here
any minute, these parents—
my first conference of the day.

Speak through me, Father.
May the words spoken here
build up and not tear down.
More than that,
may my words
engineer a bridge
between the
parents and me.

Then their child
may walk steadily across,
spanning the gulf
between his two worlds.

Cast all your anxiety on him because he cares for you.

1 Peter 5:7 NIV

Riddled with Guilt

My heart goes out
to this child's parents.
Need, complicated
by work schedules,
has caused
their plight.

They leave him
with the baby-sitter
all evening—and not
a very good one at that.

Consumed with guilt,
they sit before me,
wanting me to understand,
to bless the situation,
to remove any responsibility
they have for his education.

Their eyes beg for
me to tell them there

won't be any scars.
Their words cry out
for solutions.

I am just a servant,
Lord, a teacher.
I don't know the answers.
Nor can I give them the
Balm of Gilead.

But I can cast this
situation on you
and watch you work.

He will never let me stumble, slip, or fall. For he is
always watching, never sleeping.

Psalm 121:3, 4 LB

A Night of Firsts

Paper plate faces
fastened to
construction paper
bodies, stuffed
in last summer's
T-shirts, suffice
as replicas of
my students
sitting in
their seats.

Casting a quick
glance around
the flawless
room, I breathe
a sigh of relief.

Everything is ready.

Father, it is
Open House,
the season of
firsts—
    the first meeting
    between parents
    and teachers,
    the first of a
    new school year,
    and a time of
    first impressions.

I stand at
my post ready
to greet this
year's parents.

Calm my apprehension,
help me to forget
about putting
my best
foot forward.

Instead, let me
lose myself in
listening and
sharing hope for
a successful school year.

*The chief priests and the teachers of the law were
standing there, vehemently accusing him.*

Luke 23:10 NIV

The Stoning

This irate
parent stands
before me
flinging
accusations
like stones.

Deep within
me, a cry
arises at
the absurdity,
and I want to
call out
"Unfair!"

Somehow I
manage to
maintain my
professionalism.

I am a teacher.
I remember the
high calling
you have
given to me.

I think of
you, Jesus,
and what
you endured.

This is nothing.

With your
shield about me,
I stand until
the tirade ends,
and there
at my feet
lie the stones.

Lord, you opened the
blind man's eyes,
open this parent's
eyes to see
that the truth is
we want the
same thing.

He shall cover thee with his feathers, and under his
wings shalt thou trust.

Psalm 91:4 KJV

etting Go

She has loosened
her grip
on his hand,
and he appears
to be standing free
at the closet.

But her eyes
deny his
freedom.

Clutching,
with their
steel-gray
anxiousness,
they are
pulling him
back like a
magnet in one
of our science
experiments.

And the child,
torn between
his desire
to complete
this early
rite of passage
and his longing
to please Mom,
stands trembling.

Father, this is
not easy for
either one,
but please
let her leave.

Help her to see
that she can
give him wings,
because he is
under yours.

He heals the brokenhearted and binds up their
wounds.

Psalm 147:3 <small>NIV</small>

The Wounded

Studious
   silence,
      then—
the cloudburst.

A torrent of sobs
pours forth,
thundering with
deep, grievous pain,
gushing from a
wounded heart.

Jarred into
awareness
by the sudden
tumult,
all eyes turn
toward the frail
blond girl.

Rushing to her side,
I gather her
in my arms,
wiping her
salty tears away.

The shrill bell
signals recess,
and the others
file out.
Silently, I utter
a prayer of thanks
for the perfect timing.

She's calmer now;
the flood of words
begins.

I listen.

She is existing
in a soap-opera
atmosphere, and
the adults in her
life have the
starring roles.

I want so much
to help, but I can
offer only a solace,

a sanctuary of love
from 8 'til 3.

What then?
What about home?

There, parents blinded
by the world
meet only her
physical needs.
Daily they rob
her of ever
knowing a family
as you intended.
Open their eyes;
let them see
beyond themselves.

Father,
bind her wounds;
heal the fragments
of her heart.

Your education is your life—guard it well.

Proverbs 4:13 GNB

arents' Day

They arrive in
sets and as singles,
filling up the
arc of seats
placed in the back
of the room.

For just a second
I am overcome
with a wave of
nervousness
as I realize
I am standing
at center stage.

Like an
applause meter
registering acceptance,
their presence
is a good indicator
of the support

I will receive
throughout
the year.

But more than
that, it is a
declaration
to their children
that education
is important.

Father, thank
you for the
parents who
care enough
to make
their child
a top priority.

An anxious heart weighs a man down, but a kind word cheers him up.

Proverbs 12:25 NIV

A word aptly spoken is like apples of gold in settings of silver.

Proverbs 25:11 NIV

A *F*itting Word

Just a few
sentences
hastily written
on a half-sheet
of paper—
but my spirit soars.

Just a "Thank you,
we know you care."
What a treasure—
this note of appreciation
from a parent!

Opening my desk drawer,
I lift out the
mocha-brown file box.

As with a picture album,
I lose myself
within its contents.

Yellowed notes
start me reminiscing
about other years
and other parents
who spoke words
of affirmation.

Adding today's
gem to my collection,
I tuck away my
box of encouragement.

Father, I esteem
this treasury of words.
Bless these parents
who take the time.

There is a time for everything, and a season for every activity under heaven.

Ecclesiastes 3:1 NIV

A 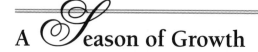eason of Growth

Like new markers
on fresh drawing
paper,
   words
      flowed
         easily
between these
parents and
me, until
I spoke the word.

Then, with a
clamourous tone,
the gate of
understanding
clanged shut.

Now, we
stand divided.

Retention.

In their eyes
it is synonymous

with shame and
failure.

In mine
it is an extension
of the learning
process, a second
chance for success.

Masking anxieties,
they voice
their concerns for
their child's
emotional
well-being.

But it goes
much deeper.
Their past
experiences and
fears have
clouded their vision,
blinding them
to what is best
for their child.

Guide me, Father.

Grant me your
key of wisdom
to unlock this
barrier.

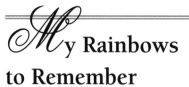

My Rainbows to Remember

Supportive parents whom I want to remember:

I will always remember these parents who have gone the extra mile:

The nicest thing a parent ever did for me:

One time I remember:

Difficult situations I have encountered regarding parents:

PART FOUR

A *Rainbow* of *Golden Moments*

I will sing to the Lord as long as I live. I will praise God to my last breath! May he be pleased by all these thoughts about him, for he is the source of all my joy.

Psalm 104:33, 34 LB

The earth is the LORD's and the fullness thereof; the world, and they that dwell therein.

Psalm 24:1 KJV

P. E.

You know I don't like
teaching P.E., Father.
Today we planned to
go outside.
I dragged my feet
as well as the parachute.
Then the door opened.

The dome of heaven,
flocked
by cotton-candy clouds,
greeted us.
Our feet danced
merrily
on rich velvet.

All of creation
was draped
in your garment
of sunlight.

The children,
marching
in a circle,
held the swirling silk,
creating
a carousel
of rainbow colors.
And their laughter,
so lilting,
floated on the wind.

Let my teaching fall like rain and my words
descend like dew, like showers on new grass, like
abundant rain on tender plants.

Deuteronomy 32:2 NIV

ranquility

Like a
dancer
tapping
out a
steady
rhythm,
the rain
beats
against the
windowpane.

The children,
intent on their work,
are lulled by
the hypnotic sound.

The scratch of
pencil meeting
paper,

the rustle
of organization,
and the faint buzz
of the clock,
amplify the mood.

For moments like this
I give thee thanks.

*And he said: "I tell you the truth, unless you change
and become like little children, you will never enter
the kingdom of heaven."*

Matthew 18:3 NIV

Reflections

Light,
  feathery,
    falling,
        it begins.

Swirling,
  spiraling,
    downward,
        it comes, faster.

Framed against
a slate-blue backdrop,
it fashions
the earth in shimmering satin.

Like glue from an overturned bottle,
word of the discovery
spreads rapidly
through the classroom.

Running to the window,
they herald it with
squeals of delight
and aerobics
only children can perform.
Their eyes
dance with anticipation.
They envision snowmen,
perhaps even Frosty himself.

Thank you, Father,
for the first snow—
and my seeing it mirrored
in the eyes of children.

The LORD shall preserve thy going out and thy com-
ing in from this time forth, and even for evermore.

Psalm 121:8 KJV

An Adventure

Feeling like Noah,
I stand here
counting students,
two by two,
as they enter
this yellow ark.

Unlike Noah,
I will have to
load them twice.
Please, Father,
cause them to
hold securely to
their partners' hands.

Parents, on their
first field trip,
chat nervously
as their eyes
search for the

cherubs assigned
to them.

Ground rules laid,
I take my
seat of authority
behind the driver.

Like a computer's,
the memory screen
of my mind
calls up the list
of our provisions.
Mentally I check
them off.

Everything is aboard.

With a panoramic glance
I make sure that
everyone is wearing
a name tag—our
guarantee that the
lost shall be found.

Turning around,
I send up a
silent plea that
everyone really did
go to the bathroom.

Go before us, Father;
grant us a safe journey
and your protection.

And Father—
make it fun!

He is always thinking about you and watching
everything that concerns you.

1 Peter 5:7 LB

The Harvest

Clouds as puffy
as cotton ready
for harvest
extend from a
cornsilk-blue
sky, providing
us with an
afternoon as
golden as the sun.

Friendly conversation
prevails as we travel
the bumpy road in
the pickup truck.
At last, we turn
onto the dirt
road, arriving at
our destination.

Crisp autumn air
tantalizes our
noses as we step
out into fields
ripe for harvest.

Crimson and mellow-
orange spheres
beckon us, and
we swiftly gather
them in.

Already I am
projecting to
Monday morning
and the delight
on each of the
children's faces
as they are presented
with their very
own pumpkins.

Father, some
would say it
was by chance
that my friend
offered me this
bounty. But I
know better.

What an awesome
God you are!
I asked for
pumpkins, and
you the Lord
of the harvest
supplied them
from your abundance.

Be full of love for others, following the example of Christ who loved you and gave himself to God as a sacrifice to take away your sins. And God was pleased, for Christ's love for you was like sweet perfume to him.

Ephesians 5:2 LB

A Sweet Fragrance

Carols set
the mood
as we sit
around the table
snipping
dried orange
peels and pine
needles.

Small hands
stir in
cinnamon
and cloves,
filling our
classroom with
the aroma of
an old-fashioned
Christmas.

Potpourri—they can
barely say it—this
gift they are creating
for their parents.

One by one
I behold their faces.
For a brief span
time appears
suspended like a
golden moment
captured by
a still photo.

I am keenly
aware that I
am being
allowed to sample
a different kind
of Christmas
potpourri,
a heavenly scent
composed of
    angelic beams
    radiating from
    glowing faces,
    eyes aflame
    with hope,
    pureness of hearts,
    a giving of oneself,
    and echoes of laughter.

Father, may they
take this sweet
fragrance of you
back into their
homes as they
give their gifts.

For this moment
of Christmas and
the closeness we
share, I give
you thanks.

Bless These Days

Like the plastic
coins we use in
our math store,
I spend the
approaching days
of spring break
over and over.

Savoring each
appetizing idea,
I stretch the
course of each
delectable day.

This morning
the very air
is charged with
an electric-like
excitement.

Three o'clock,
and there is
no containing
the eagerness.
Good-byes are
shouted along
with best wishes.

A yellow
freight train
loaded with
precious cargo
pulls out,
leaving only
my co-workers
singing their
song of release.

Glancing around,
my view spans an
earth awakening
to spring. With
my heart light,
my feet leap in
a freedom dance,
and I give a
squeal of delight.

My day has arrived!

Father, bless these
days of my spring break.

Just as Christ was raised from the dead through the glory of the Father, we too may live a new life.

Romans 6:4 NIV

ew Life

Rainbow colors
fizz into
brilliance,
tinting the
clear liquid
in the
hodgepodge
containers.

Just as color
added to paint
marbles outward,
excitement ripples
from the table
in the center
of the room.

Eggs designed
with crayon
markings and

dyed in hues
mixed by
creative artists
multiply in
assembly-line fashion,
proclaiming proudly
from their cartons,
There is new life!

Father, for this
egg coloring
ritual and these
little ones
you have entrusted
to me—I give
thanks.

Guide each one
of them until
they find new
life in you.

I asked God from the wealth of his glory to give
you power through his Spirit to be strong in your
inner selves, and I pray that Christ will make his
home in your hearts through faith. I pray that you
may have your roots and foundation in love.

Ephesians 3:16, 17 GNB

A *Time* of Planting

Cups of soil
line the windowsill
promising that soon,
plants will emerge.

The students,
charged with supplying
the nourishment
for their plants,
check them continually
through eyes of faith.

Father, thank you
for this lesson,
for in my teaching
you have taught me.
Now I see that my

students are seedlings
you have placed
within my care.
You have assigned me
the responsibility of
nurturing them.

I pray that the
sunlight of knowledge
will flood their
minds, and the rain
of discontent will
make them delve
more deeply until they
are rooted academically.

But even more,
I pray that you
will spiritually
nourish them until
they take hold,
becoming rooted
and grounded in
your love.

Be happy. Grow in Christ. Pay attention to what I have said. Live in harmony and peace. And may the God of love and peace be with you.

2 Corinthians 13:11 LB

The Farewell

We have marked
off the days,
and now that
the last one
has arrived,
our emotions
are like a
kaleidoscope,
constantly
changing design
as we rotate
from gladness
to sadness and
back again.

Grocery sacks
stuffed with
memorabilia
of the year

gone by,
testify
of what our
hearts already
know—
it will never
be the same.

Hugs to last
a summer
reassure us.
Our bond will remain strong.
Promises of hope
for chance meetings
abound.

Reminiscent of
Times Square on
New Year's Eve,
someone begins
a countdown
of seconds.
The final bell
sounds, accompanied
by proclamations
of joy.

Buses loaded,
they pull out
with horns

honking wildly
in the classic
year-end
falderal.
Protruding arms
wave a final
good-bye.

Misty eyed,
I wave until
distance diminishes
the buses to
matchbox size.

Father, you
who are the
Creator of all
our emotions,
understand
how it is that
my heart sings
at the thought
of a brand new
summer and at
the same time,
cries, for I
have just said
good-bye to a
part of myself.

Guide our paths,
Father, causing
them to cross
throughout the
years.

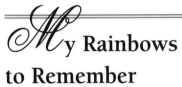
My Rainbows
to Remember

My favorite golden moments:

A golden moment surrounding a holiday:

One time I remember:

My thoughts about the beginning of the school year:

My thoughts about the end of the school year: